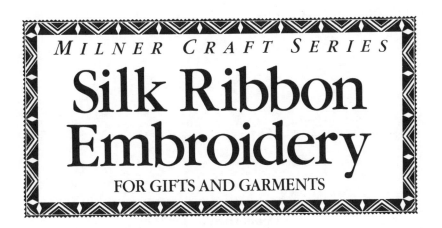

MILNER CRAFT SERIES

Silk Ribbon Embroidery

FOR GIFTS AND GARMENTS

JENNY BRADFORD

SALLY MILNER PUBLISHING

First published in 1990 by
Sally Milner Publishing Pty Ltd
558 Darling Street
Rozelle NSW 2039 Australia

Reprinted 1990, 1991 (twice), 1992 (three times),
1993

© Jenny Bradford, 1990

Design by David Constable
Photography by Andre Martin
Typeset in 12/13 Goudy by
Asset Typesetting Pty Ltd, Sydney
Printed in Australia by Impact Printing, Melbourne

National Library of Australia Cataloguing-in-Publication data:

Bradford, Jenny, 1936-
   Silk Ribbon embroidery for gifts and garments.

   ISBN 1 86351 051 6.

   1.Embroidery. 2. Ribbon work. I. Title. (Series : Milner craft
   series).

746.44

ACKNOWLEDGEMENTS

I would like to thank my friends, students and the many people I meet in my travels who by their interest and enthusiasm have encouraged me to go on exploring this field of embroidery.

Special thanks to Lois White for designing and making the beautiful bridal hat; my son Terry for his help in preparing the manuscript; finally my husband Don, who should be listed as co-author for the contribution he makes to my work, assisting with the manuscript and drawing all the diagrams.

Jenny Bradford, 1990

CONTENTS

INTRODUCTION

When I first started working with silk ribbon I had no idea what a fascinating and totally absorbing form of embroidery it would prove to be. The rapid increase in popularity of this craft has to be due to the fact that many embroiderers are also finding this to be the case.

In this, my third book on the subject, I have set out to introduce new techniques, stitches and designs in order to expand the scope and possibilities of Silk Ribbon Embroidery.

The stitches used are all traditional embroidery stitches ideally suited to ribbon work and complimentary to those chosen for the work represented in my earlier publications.

The emphasis is on new techniques all of which are described in careful detail making the book ideal for beginners as well as more experienced embroiderers.

All the designs illustrated are worked with variations of just six simple stitches. Most are washable and can be used to decorate clothing.

Detailed instructions together with full size patterns, where applicable, for all gift ideas are included, together with suggestions for suitable garment adaptations.

CHAPTER 1

MATERIALS

RIBBON

Silk ribbon has been used for all the projects in this book. It is softer and more pliable than any other type of ribbon available. As a result of this the work produced can be extremely fine and delicate.

Pure silk ribbon is currently available in approximately 185 shades in 4 mm width, 73 shades in 2 mm width and 30 shades in 7 mm width. It can be purchased from specialist embroidery and craft shops.

There is a synthetic ribbon very similar in appearance to the 4 mm wide silk ribbon but this is not as widely available as the pure silk and the colour range is very limited.

The difference between the two ribbon types can be likened to that between natural fibre fabrics which crush much more readily than synthetic fabrics. The synthetic ribbon has much more 'bounce' than the silk and therefore will not compact to the same degree, resulting in coarser work. This may be an advantage in some designs, however the main criterion for your choice of ribbon should be that it is the one with which you personally enjoy working, as that is usually the ribbon that will suit your own style best.

This last statement also applies to the width of the ribbons selected for a design. The scale of a design can be increased by using wider ribbons, or decreased by using narrower ribbon. I find so much variation in individual student's work, due to natural differences in working tension, that the best advice I can give is for you to experiment with the various widths until you are satisfied with the results.

NEEDLES

A selection of crewel, tapestry, chenille and straw needles in various sizes will be most useful.

Crewel or embroidery needles have a sharp point, a short shaft and a long slender eye and can be purchased in a packet of assorted sizes 3 to 9.

Tapestry needles have a blunt point, short shaft and long enlarged eye. Also available in assorted size packets. Sizes 18 to 24 will be most useful.

Chenille needles are very similar in appearance to tapestry needles except that they have a sharp point. Also available in assorted sizes from 18 to 24. In all cases the higher the number the finer the needle.

Straw needles have sharp points and fine eyes in long constant diameter shafts. Available in assorted sizes from 3 to 10, this type of needle is excellent for working colonial knots, and other embroidery highlights, in thread. The very finest of these is also excellent for sewing on beads as they are stronger and more durable than beading needles.

The choice of needle depends on the following:

● The type of stitch to be executed.

Any stitch requiring the needle to pass *between* a ribbon stitch and the base fabric should be worked with a tapestry needle to avoid snagging either the ribbon or the base fabric.

- The type of fabric you are working on.
  The background fabric may influence the choice of needle; a tapestry needle may pull threads on fine silk or be hard to get through closely woven fabrics.

- The width of ribbon used.
  The eye of the needle must be large enough to accommodate the ribbon comfortably and make a hole large enough for the ribbon to pass through easily.

A guide for maintaining even sized loops when working flowers in looped straight stitch is useful. It is possible to work these loops over a large tapestry needle but this requires accurate judgement to maintain even length. A more accurate guide is to use a small section of a knitting needle, 7 cm (3 inches) is ample, provided it can be cut and smoothed properly. Other alternatives are cable knitting needles or the end pieces from circular knitting needles which can be cut from the flexible wire section and smoothed with sandpaper or a nail file. I use a size 5 mm cable needle for 7 mm ribbon roses or poppies and also 2 mm ribbon daisies.

THREADS

A wide variety of embroidery threads may be successfully used in combination with silk ribbon. The main consideration is to choose between a shiny or a dull thread.

Stranded threads such as Soie d'Algere (a seven strand silk thread), stranded cotton and Marlitt (a very high sheen viscose thread) are all useful. Even a single strand of these threads may be too heavy for some flower centres, in which case machine embroidery thread will prove useful.

FABRICS

A wide variety of fabrics are suitable for ribbon embroidery provided they are not abrasive in any way. The projects in this book have been worked on shantung, silks, cotton, linen, synthetics and hand knitted garments.

Some fine and most loosely woven fabrics may require a stabiliser in the form of a second layer of the same fabric, silk organza, fine cotton or fine batting.

Suitability of design and stitch choice play an important part in the success of a project and should always be taken into consideration when planning your work.

EMBROIDERY HOOPS

I find many students dislike the thought of having to use an embroidery hoop, as I did myself at first. It is, however, essential to use one for most ribbon work.

One reason many students find hoops clumsy and awkward is that there is a tendency to use too large a hoop. For this reason I prefer the small plastic and metal spring hoops that are available in 7.5 cm (3 inch) and 10.5 cm (4⅛ inch) diameter. These hoops are easy to move around and there is a section of fabric between the spring handles that does not get clipped into the frame. If the fabric is positioned carefully finished embroidery can be passed through this section without squashing it in the frame.

The main reason for using a small hoop is that it is necessary to be able to reach the stitching area with both hands in order to manipulate the ribbon correctly.

Keeping the fabric taut in a frame makes the process of 'spreading the ribbon' easier and greatly assists in working flowers evenly.

FABRIC MARKING PENS

There are two types — water soluble and fadeable. Some people prefer not to use these pens as the long term effect of the chemicals in them is unknown. However I find them very useful for putting very light guide marks when positioning the main flowers in a design.

KEY FOR ALL DIAGRAMS IN PROJECTS

o   Colonial knot

|| Straight stitch rose buds

0   Single rosette stitch buds

    Pearl stitch flowers

    Rosette stitch flowers

    3 petal flowers

    4 petal straight stitch flowers

    5 petal straight stitch flowers

    Rose

    Poppy or buttercup

   Daisy

CHAPTER 2

BASIC TECHNIQUES
AND HELPFUL HINTS FOR EMBROIDERY WITH RIBBON

The ribbon is used in the needle as a thread, however, because it is flat rather than cylindrical, it is necessary to follow some basic rules in order to work the ribbon successfully.

The length of ribbon used in the needle may vary according to the stitches being worked. Because over worked and worn ribbon is much harder to manipulate I suggest using short 30 cm (12 inch) lengths. This is particularly important where 'spreading the ribbon' is an essential part of the technique.

THREADING THE NEEDLE

The nature of the ribbon allows it to be threaded and locked into the eye of the needle thus making the maximum use of the ribbon length. This prevents accidental loss of the needle but makes unthreading difficult. The use of a separate needle for each colour being used is therefore recommended.

To thread the needle, pass the end of the ribbon through the eye of the needle. Thread this end of the ribbon onto the point of the needle, piercing the ribbon about 12 mm (½ inch) from the end. Pull back on the long end of the ribbon until the ribbon locks firmly into the eye of the needle.

STARTING

Leave a small tail hanging at the back of the work. Pierce this tail with the needle as the first stitch is taken. This stitch can be the first one of the design or taken as a tiny backstitch to be hidden under the subsequent stitching. Once some stitching has been done new threads can be introduced by weaving behind these stitches on the back of the work, however care must be taken not to distort the surface stitches during this process.

Be careful if you skip from one part of the design to another that the ribbons will not show through when the work is finished.

FINISHING

Weave the ribbon in behind the stitching if possible or cut off leaving a tail to be caught in as the next thread is started, as with 'starting'.

MANIPULATING THE RIBBON

It is impossible to over-emphasise the importance of learning how to manipulate the ribbon correctly.

There is little point in using ribbon for embroidery if it is going to end up looking more like thread than ribbon. The simple basic techniques described here should be practised with care until they become an automatic part of your routine stitching. Learning to perfect the stitches will save time, effort and ribbon.

Most of the stitches worked with ribbon require the full face of the ribbon to be laid down smoothly without twists. The following points will help ensure this:

- Keep ribbon lengths short, as recommended. It is easier to see and remove twists from shorter lengths.
- Hold the ribbon flat against the fabric under the left thumb while you take the stitch. Keeping the thumb in place while you tighten the thread firmly over the thumb will, in most cases, remove all the twists from the ribbon, enabling the stitch to be completed smoothly.
- If preferred, a large tapestry needle can be used instead of the left thumb to tension the ribbon.

The point of this process is to remove twists before the stitch is completed. Poking and prodding with a needle after the stitch is set will snag and fray the ribbon. If you do need to adjust a stitch, use a tapestry needle to loosen the ribbon carefully before repeating the process.

SPREADING THE RIBBON

Spreading the ribbon is also very important for some stitches.

This technique is designed to give an even spread of the ribbon as it passes through the base fabric. Allowing the edges of the ribbon to fold over or under means that the stitch, when completed, will not show the full face of the ribbon.

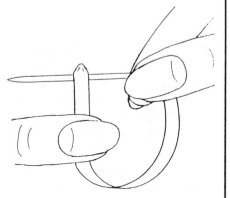

- Bring the needle up at the required point.
- Hold the ribbon flat under the left thumb.
- Slide the needle under the ribbon and, using a gentle upward pressure on the ribbon with the needle, slide it back to the exit point.

If the ribbon fails to spread evenly, turn it over and try again as it may be twisted where it passes through the base fabric.

This process should not be difficult providing the needle used is large enough to create a hole of sufficient size to accommodate the ribbon easily.

CHAPTER 3

STITCHES
AND THEIR USES

The stitches detailed in this chapter have many different applications. The more firmly twisted or knotted the ribbon during the working, the more durable the embroidery will be. It is therefore essential to choose stitches with these properties for projects requiring washable and hard-wearing forms of the embroidery.

More delicate interpretations of some stitches may be used on projects such as box tops, pictures, cards, etc which one would not normally expect to launder.

There are endless possibilities and variations using these few simple stitches, taking into consideration the fact that each stitch varies in size and character when worked in each of the three different width ribbons.

I recommend practising the stitches on a sampler to establish tension and technique before starting a project. A degree of difficulty is given for each stitch and variations of that stitch. Beginners should start with the easy classifications and progress gradually to more advanced techniques. The more experienced workers should be able to select any technique provided the instructions are followed carefully and due care and attention is given to 'manipulating the ribbon' (see page 6) where applicable.

FLOWERS

If a specific variety of flower is to be depicted care must be taken to choose a colour as true as possible to the flower variety. The shape and number of petals worked is also important as is the size in relation to any other flowers used in the design.

Many flowers have an uneven number of petals, generally five, rather than an even number such as four or six. Beginners will find it easier to arrange an even number of petals in a circle, but five are not difficult with practice.

To arrange five petals evenly around the flower centre the following image may help. Imagine the flower as a clock face and position petals as shown in the diagram.

Working the petals so that they radiate evenly from the centre of the flower can be a problem. I find the following method helps to prevent petals from slipping sideways and distorting the shape of the flower.

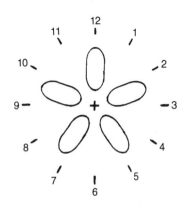

- Work the first petal at twelve o'clock, then bring the needle back through the fabric at the base of the next petal.

- Now *turn the work* so that the petal to be worked is now in the twelve o'clock position. Complete this petal and position the needle at the base of the next petal before turning the work again.

Working each petal in the same position makes judging the length easier and ensures even radiation from the centre.

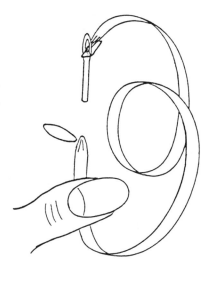

FLAT STRAIGHT STITCH — EASY

This stitch is used for rosebuds, small flowers and leaves. It is very effective and easy to work provided sufficient care and attention are given to spreading the ribbon at the start of each stitch and removing any twists from the ribbon before tightening the stitch.

- Bring the needle up at point A.

- Hold the ribbon flat against the fabric, under the left thumb, directly opposite the required position of the stitch.

- Spread the ribbon.

- Making the stitch the required length, pass the needle down through the fabric at point B.

- Keep the left thumb in position as long as possible, forming the ribbon loop over it. Pulling the ribbon firmly at this point should remove the twists from the ribbon. Slide the thumb from the loop and gently tighten the stitch to the desired tension.

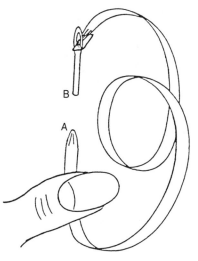

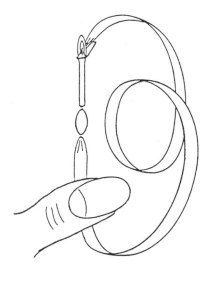

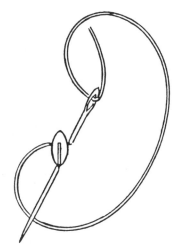

Rosebuds — easy and washable

Rosebuds are very easy to work using 2, 4 or 7 mm ribbon, depending on the scale of the design. Overstitching with embroidery thread makes these flowers strong, durable and washable.

- Working from the base to the tip of the bud, lay a single straight stitch of length equal to the width of the ribbon being used.

- Cover this stitch with a second straight stitch starting immediately below and extending just beyond the tip of the first stitch.

- Using stranded thread, single strand for 2 and 4 mm ribbon, two strands for 7 mm ribbon, come up at the base of the bud and take a single straight stitch two thirds of the way up the centre of the ribbon stitch. Bring the needle back up on the left hand side of the bud, in line with this point. Take the needle down on the right hand side of the bud and out at the base, with the thread looped under the needle (see diagram). Anchor with a tiny straight stitch or use this thread to form a stem for the bud.

Small Flowers — washable
4 petals — easy; 5 petals — difficult

- Mark a small dot for the flower centre, the finer the ribbon the smaller the dot required.

- Keeping the base of the petals close to the marked spot, position four or five petals as shown in the diagram on page 8.

A good guide to the petal size is to make them the same length as the width of ribbon used.

Remember to turn the work as described on page 6.

Leaves

Good variation in the shape and size of straight stitch leaves can be achieved by varying the width of ribbon and the length of stitches used. Extra strength and durability can be achieved with the addition of a vein worked down the centre of the stitch with embroidery thread.

Twists and folds can be achieved by using matching embroidery thread to hold the ribbon in place, allowing the stitch to change direction. See diagram.

LOOPED STRAIGHT STITCH — ADVANCED

This stitch is used for briar roses, poppies, buttercups and daisies. The flowers have a lovely three-dimensional quality but are rather fragile. Washing and ironing is not to be recommended. They are most effective used on box tops, jewellery, gift cards, pictures, etc.

They are more difficult to work than most of the other flowers because the petal loops are not secure and can easily be distorted until after the centres have been worked.

You may need a second tapestry needle or a cable knitting needle to slip through the ribbon loops to hold them evenly as you work.

Briar Roses and Poppies

To create briar roses or poppies using 7 mm ribbon and a large chenille needle:

- Mark a small circle.

- Work a straight stitch, coming up at the petal base and going down about 3 mm (⅛ inch) from this point, adjusting the loop over the spare needle — a size 5 mm cable needle.

- Work a second loop over the needle without removing the needle from the first loop.

- Slip the first petal off the needle before working the third petal. Note that keeping the previous petal on the spare needle each time helps to avoid pulling the petal loop tight accidentally.

- When all petals are worked, thread a fine straw needle with machine embroidery thread, yellow for roses, black or green for poppies.

- Work the centres in pistol stitch, see page 20. Arranging the petals as you work, make one pistol stitch down the centre of each petal to hold them firmly in position.

- Continue working pistol stitches of various lengths around the centre, over the base of the petals. Fill the centre with colonial knots.

Buttercups, small roses and poppies are worked in the same way using 4 mm ribbon and starting with a smaller centre, with the loops made over a size 3 mm cable needle.

Daisies

These are worked in 2 mm ribbon and need many more loops to complete the flower.

- Draw a small circle about 4 mm (¹⁄₆ inch) in diameter and start the petals close to the centre. This is so that the centre of the flower can be worked over the base of the petals in order to hold them firmly in place.

- Eight petals form the base row, evenly spaced around the centre circle. Work a second row of petals in the gaps between the first row, adding as many petals as are needed to fill all spaces.

- Using gold or brown embroidery thread, work a circle of colonial knots for the flower centre, working well over the base of the petals to secure them firmly.

WHIPPED RUNNING STITCH — EASY — WASHABLE

This stitch is used for outline work and is based on a line of even running stitches placed along the design lines.

The surface stitches should be even in length and each stitch should be slightly longer than the width of the ribbon being used.

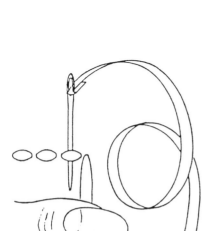

The gaps between each stitch should be as small as you can comfortably make them depending on the width of the ribbon and the type of fabric being used.

- Using a crewel needle work a row of running stitches along the design lines. It is not necessary to worry about spreading the ribbon for this step.

- Using a tapestry needle, commence the wrapping ribbon just before the start of the first running stitch, spread the ribbon and with the ribbon below the needle pass the needle down under the first running stitch. Repeat a second time through the same stitch. Tighten this stitch to wrap firmly around the foundation stitch.

- For best results take care to remove all twists from the ribbon and ensure that the full face of the ribbon wraps flat around the running stitches.

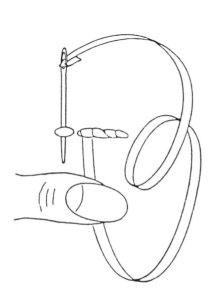

- Pass the needle under the second running stitch in the same way but take care not to pull this stitch too firmly or allow the ribbon to twist.

- Firmly wrap this foundation stitch a second time as before.

Continue this sequence along the line of running stitches alternating tightly wrapped stitches around the foundation stitching with more loosely wrapped stitches between each foundation stitch.

WHIPPED STITCH— USED FOR ROSES AND OTHER FLOWERS
— EASY WASHABLE

Similar in character to the whipped running stitch but each straight stitch is wrapped as it is laid on the fabric.

- Work a straight stitch the required length. A-B.
- Bring the needle back to the surface at point C.
- Wrap the foundation stitch twice, working towards point B.
- Repeat wrapping process again covering the first wraps and moving back towards point A.
- Anchor the stitch by passing the needle to the back of the work where the last wrap stitch finishes.
- It is essential to eliminate all twists from the wrapping ribbon at all times.
- The completed stitch can be encouraged to curve gently by adjusting the point at which it is anchored. If it is placed directly under the stitch the whipped stitch will remain straight; if it is placed at the edge of the stitch, as shown in the diagram, it will pull the whipped stitch in a curve towards that point.

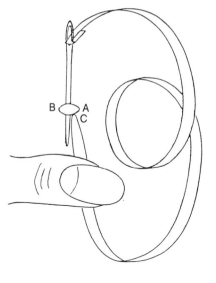

Both whipped running stitch and whipped stitch are easier to work if the hoop is resting on the table or your lap, in order to free the left hand to assist in manipulating the ribbon.

Slipping the needle into the loop as the ribbon is tightened will help remove the twists and assist in accurate placement of the wrap stitches.

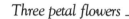

Three petal flowers

These flowers are not intended to represent any specific type of flower, so choice of colour and ribbon size will depend entirely on the type of design chosen. They are comparatively quick to work, economical on ribbon and will wash and wear well.

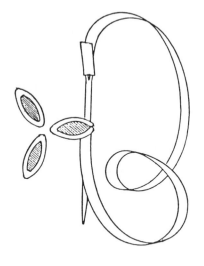

- Commence with a tiny dot for the centre.
- Work three whipped stitches in a darker shade of ribbon at twelve, four and eight o'clock.
- Using a lighter shade of ribbon work one whipped stitch on each side of each dark stitch, first on the left then on the right, extending them to just beyond the tip of the first stitch. Work all the wraps on the outside stitches in the one direction from the base to the tip of the petals, taking the final wrap of the second outside stitch over the point of the first outside stitch to draw them together.
- Work a single colonial knot in 2 mm ribbon for the flower centre.

Roses — easy

These roses are very firm and strong and wash and wear well. The stitches are positioned in the same way as they are for bullion roses. They are quick and easy to work and can be worked using any width ribbon in one, two or three shades.

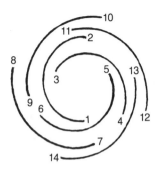

- Work a single colonial knot for the centre, using the darkest shade of ribbon. The use of a large tapestry needle will give a nice cup to the centre of the knot. Do not tighten the ribbon too much when working the knot.

- Work three whipped stitches in a clockwise direction around the centre knot, using ribbon of a lighter shade if desired. Position the stitches as shown in the diagram. Bring the needle up between the row you are working and the centre knot, half way along the stitch just completed. Anchor each stitch into a slight curve.
- Work four or five whipped stitches around the previous row. The ribbon can, once again, be a lighter shade. Position these stitches in the same way as in the previous row, starting each new stitch halfway back and on the inside of the previously worked stitch. Anchor each stitch into a slight curve around the previous row.

ROSETTE CHAIN — WASHABLE

A traditional embroidery stitch, this versatile stitch makes a pretty braid type edging to collars and cuffs when worked in a continuous line. It can also be used to form tiny flower buds by working each stitch individually or as a flower by working the stitches in a circle. It is not necessary to spread the ribbon for this stitch.

- Working from right to left and using a tapestry needle bring the needle up at point A, form a small anti-clockwise loop of ribbon, passing the needle through the fabric above the loop at B, level with but to the left of point A.

- Bring the needle back to the surface at point C inside the loop of ribbon and directly below point B. The distance between points B and C should be slightly less than the width of ribbon used.

- Tighten the stitch before passing the needle upwards under the ribbon between point A and B.

- To work a line or circle of stitches, form the ribbon loop at this point and insert the needle at point B, the required distance away from the preceding stitch.

- For individual buds finish each stitch by passing the needle to the back of the work between points A and B.

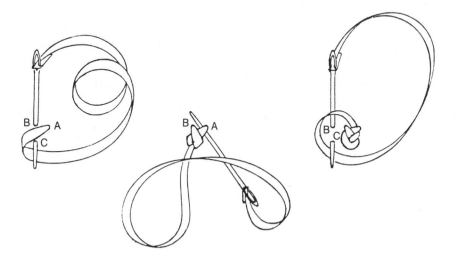

Lavender — easy

Individual stitches of rosette chain can be used to represent stems of lavender.

The ribbon is firmly twisted and therefore may be used in wash and wear situations.

- Using stranded embroidery thread, work the stems in couching.

- Using 2 mm ribbon, thread a fine tapesty needle with one length each of pale green and lavender ribbon.

- Holding the work upside down work a row of single rosette chain stitches up each stem, starting each stitch on the stem.

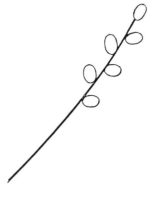

Pussy Willow — easy

- Work twig style stems in whipped running stitch using brown 4 mm ribbon.

- Using 2 mm ribbon in cream, work single rosette chain stitches at intervals along the stems.

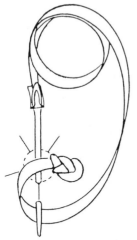

Rosette Chain Flowers — easy

These may be worked in a variety of ways using 2, 4 or 7 mm ribbon, single or double strand. Double strands can be of shaded or contrasting colours.

- Draw a circle for the centre of the flower. Make a tiny mark on edge of the circle for the base of each petal.

- Work rosette chain in to a circle, starting the base of each petal at the marked points.

- Work colonial knots for the centre of each flower.

HAT BOX, HORSESHOE, GIFT CARD AND WEDDING HAT

ALICE BAND, EARRINGS, GIFT CARD, WIRED FLOWERS AND LEAVES

STEPS FOR HEART ON FRONT COVER

BOXES, METAL, WOODEN, RECESSED LIDS

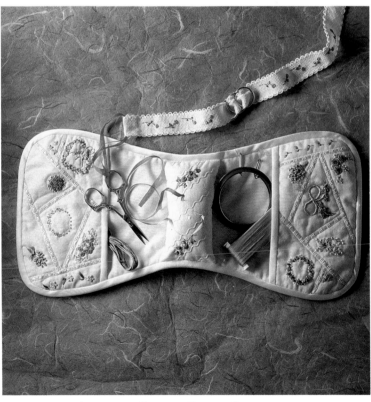

ARMCHAIR SEWING CADDY, CHATELAINE

BAG WITH BEADS

SLIPPERS, CHRISTMAS GIFTS, GIFT CARDS AND TAGS

DRESS WITH EMBROIDERED COLLAR, BUCKLE AND SLEEVES

BABIES' GARMENTS, COLLAR, KNITTED ITEMS, BOOTIES AND GIFT CARD

VEST

DETAIL OF HEART ON BACK OF VEST

MINIATURE CUSHIONS AND BEDSPREAD

PEARL STITCH

Traditionally worked as a line stitch this stitch can be used for outlining or defining a pattern and when the stitches are worked close together it resembles a string of pearls. It is also possible to work this stitch in a tight circle to form very pretty tiny flowers. The stitch is worked from right to left and is best worked with a tapestry needle.

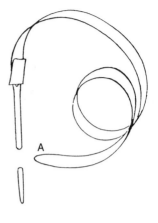

- Bring the needle up at point A.

- Take a tiny vertical stitch to the left of point A.

- Pass the needle under the small slanting stitch thus formed.

- Ensure the slanting stitch is tightened before adjusting the tension of the wrap stitch which looks better if left a little more relaxed.

- To work the stitch into a four petal flower, position the straight stitches at three, six and nine and twelve o'clock. Commence at the tip of the three o'clock petal and make the small vertical stitch at six o'clock [2 to 3]. Wrap the stitch as described.

- Repeat with straight stitches at nine [4 to 5], twelve [6 to 7] and three o'clock, [8 to 9].

- Take the needle to the back of the work [10].

It is important when working flowers to keep the wrap thread twist free and leave the tension relaxed.

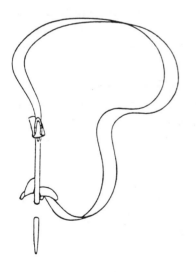

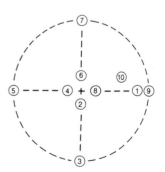

COLONIAL KNOTS — WASHABLE

I find it very difficult to do any design without including some colonial knots. They are particularly attractive when worked in ribbon and can be used as tiny rosebuds, baby's breath and generally make an excellent fill in to the background.

Varying the size of the needle can affect the look of a colonial knot considerably and I suggest you experiment with both the size of the needle and the width of ribbon used. Basically a fatter needle will produce a knot with a larger hole in the centre, which can look very pretty when used for the centre of a rose or as a miniature bud.

The knot will have a better shape if the ribbon is kept flat as it is picked up on the needle and not allowed to twist or fold.

Maintaining a flexible, relaxed wrist is the key to easy execution of colonial knots allowing easy change of direction as the ribbon is picked up on the needle.

- Bring the needle up through the fabric and hold the ribbon between the thumb and first finger of the left hand, leaving a loop approximately 8 cm (3 inches) in length.
- Slide the first finger of the right hand under this loop and 'sandwich' the ribbon between this finger and the needle, which should be pointing away from you, and hook the needle under the ribbon (figure 1).
- Turn the needle anti-clockwise through 180 degrees and hook the needle under the ribbon again (figure 2).
- Return the needle in a clockwise direction to the original position and pass the needle back through the fabric close to but not through the original exit hole (figure 3).

To produce well-shaped, even knots always neaten the ribbon around the shaft of the needle, while the needle is held in a perpendicular position in the fabric, before completing the last step.

HALF COLONIAL KNOTS

These knots are smaller than a full colonial knot, similar in size to a french knot but more firmly twisted.

It is the second half of a full colonial knot.

- Bring the needle up through the fabric.
- With the needle pointing towards you, pick up the ribbon as shown in figure 2.
- Finish as before.

Carnations

These pretty flowers are easy to make and can be used in two ways but washing and ironing are not to be recommended.

They are made before being applied to the fabric and can either be sewn on to the base fabric or attached where required with fabric glue.

- To make each flower take two 10 cm (4 inch) lengths of two shades of 7 mm ribbon.
- Lay the two ribbons together with the darker shade on top and allowing 1 mm of the lighter ribbon to show along the bottom edge.
- Using a matching thread, run a gathering thread along the bottom edge of the darker ribbon through both thicknesses (see diagram).
- Pull up the gathers and tie securely into a tight circle, taking care to leave the raw edges of the ends of the ribbon at the back of the flower behind the darker ribbon.
- Re-thread the needle with one end of the thread and bring the needle up through the centre of the flower and sew on tiny beads for the flower centre if required.
- If sewing the flowers onto the background, leave the ends of the gathering threads attached for this purpose.
- If the flowers are to be glued in place, knot the threads again after attaching the beads and trim the ends.
- If desired seal the raw edges of the ribbon with a light application of fabric glue to prevent fraying.

THREAD STITCHES

FEATHER STITCH

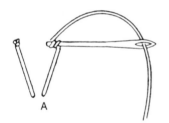

This stitch is useful for outlining a shape that will be embroidered with a random selection of flowers — for example the heart pictured on the cover. It can also be very useful as a background fill of fern type leaves.

- Bring the needle up at A at the top of the line to be followed.
- Take the needle down through the fabric below this point and to the right of the line.
- Slant the needle down slightly and bring it back to the surface on the line with the thread looped under the needle. Pull the needle through.
- Repeat the stitch inserting the needle to the left of the centre line. Continue working down the line, alternating the stitches from side to side.
- This is a 'one way' stitch. Take care that all the stems point in the right direction on a design.

PISTIL STITCH

Worked in one or two strands of embroidery thread.

- Bring the needle up at point A.
- Pick up the thread once or twice around the needle.
- Return the needle to the back of the work the required distance from point A, pulling the thread taut around the needle as the needle is passed through the fabric.

COUCHING

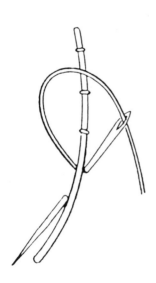

It is easy to work fine stems with a natural curve using couching.

Very short stems can be worked with a single needle, however for longer stems greater control is maintained by using two needles. The first needle carries a thread of suitable thickness for the required stem, usually one to four strands of embroidery thread. The second carries a single matching strand of the same thread.

- Using the first needle, come up at one end of the line to be covered and go down at the other. Anchor this needle out of the way.
- Bring the second needle up close to the starting point of the first thread and work tiny, straight, holding stitches across the main thread, curving the main thread as desired.

LADDER STITCH

This is a simple and neat way to close seams left open for turning and invisibly joining two sections together in box construction.

Pick up a few threads of fabric along the seam line on one side then pick up the same distance along the seam line on the other side of the opening. The cross over thread represents the rung of the ladder, the pick up sections the side supports.

As long as a strong enough thread is used, several stitches can be worked and then tightened really firmly to pull the two sides together securely.

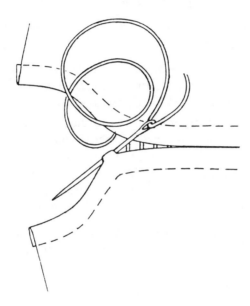

CHAPTER 4

PREPARING
TO WORK A PROJECT

Careful consideration of the many factors that influence the end results of your project before starting will often help to avoid the frustration and disappointment that results from a project that turns out not quite right.

CHOICE OF FABRIC

This is particularly relevant to the final construction techniques. When choosing the fabric ask yourself the following questions:

- Is the fabric the best weight for the project? A medium to heavy fabric weight is ideal for a handbag, however the same fabric may be very difficult and bulky to handle when covering a hairband or working a box top.

- If the project will require laundering are the laundering requirements of the fabric suitable? It is a pity to ruin the lovely three-dimensional properties of silk ribbon embroidery by choosing fabrics that require heavy use of an iron. For example, handkerchief linen is a very beautiful and popular choice of fabric for collars, however it requires the use of a very hot iron and firm pressing after laundering. I prefer to use a fabric that has drip dry qualities and does not require so much ironing.

The ideal way of pressing ribbon embroidery is to press it face down over a soft towel. The use of starch spray does not affect the ribbon in any way.

CHOICE OF STITCHES

Whether the item you are embroidering will require laundering or not is an important consideration when choosing stitches.

All stitches and flowers described previously are interchangeable. For example, designs shown using looped stitch flowers could all be worked using roses or straight stitch flowers for projects where laundering will be required. The choice of flat straight stitch flowers will ensure that the embroidery is not spoilt on fabrics such as handkerchief linen that require very firm pressing.

The amount of time you wish to spend on a project is an important consideration when making your choice of stitches and complexity of design. Projects such as Christmas decorations, cards and gift tags should be quick and simple. A minimum amount of embroidery combined with a clever use of fabric, lace, braid and beads can make such projects fun to do and a pleasure to give.

CARE OF SILK RIBBON EMBROIDERY

The manufacturers claim that the ribbon is colourfast and in the main I have found this to be so, however I have had colour leakage from some of the stronger colours such as red, blue, purple and black.

My recommendation is that the stronger colours are tested first if they are to be used on pale backgrounds. Work a few stitches in the required colours and wash in the same way as the finished article will be handled.

Do not use detergents but choose a mild soap recommended for delicate fabrics.

PREPARING THE FABRIC

1 Pre-wash all fabrics that will be laundered later.

2 When using lightweight fabrics it may provide a better working surface to back the fabric with a layer of lightweight batting. This will hide all ribbon tails that might show through from the back of the work. See details of the various projects.

The use of batting can also turn a lightweight fabric into a medium or heavyweight fabric, particularly if it is quilted.

Quilting also reduces the amount of ironing required on some fabric.

3 Quilting your own fabric can be very effective and not difficult if the following points are observed.

- Refer to the instructions provided with your sewing machine, or ask your machine supplier, for details of how to set up your particular brand of machine to use a quilting guide. This guide, which is usually included in the accessory kit provided with the machine, is adjustable and is set to the required width to ensure even stitching without having to mark the fabric.
- Fabrics should be pinned together and the pins removed as you progress across the piece.
- The easiest way to work is on the diagonal as this makes the first row across one corner very short, and an extra bonus is the fact that any slight discrepancies in spacing that may occur are not as obvious.
- Single needle and normal sewing thread can be used for this quilting, however very interesting effects can be gained using a twin needle, machine embroidery thread and one of the fancy embroidery stitches available on your machine. The main point to remember is that when using a twin needle in conjunction with a zigzag setting the setting must not be too wide (about half way is the maximum on my Bernina) or the needle will hit the foot.
- Always allow enough fabric to re-cut the pattern pieces after quilting is finished.

4 Transferring the design to the fabric.

It is essential to have a good outline of the design on the fabric and a clear definition line of the shape of the finished item in order to position the design correctly.

I find the most successful and permanent way of doing this is to use a method I favour for applique work. See *Silk Ribbon Embroidery 2* by Jenny Bradford, published by Greenhouse.

- Trace or draw the required lines of the design on to thin paper, such as computer paper.
- Position the paper on the *wrong* side of the fabric, laying batting, if used, between the paper and the fabric.
- Use matching thread as fine as possible (machine embroidery thread is ideal), stitch along the marked design lines from the wrong side. Note that tight curves will be easier to follow if you use a small stitch.

- Tear away the paper. Trim thread ends. When embroidering over these lines work just to one side of the stitching.

5 For small projects such as box tops and jewellery it is easier to work the embroidery before cutting out the final shape, to provide sufficient fabric for securing into the embroidery frame.

CHAPTER 5

PROJECTS AND DESIGNS

BAGS

There are many patterns for bags available. These can be found in the accessory section of the large dressmaking pattern books, patchwork and other craft publications. The handbag pictured in this book is made using a pattern and aluminium spring frame produced by Ghee's of the USA.

The panel carrying the embroidery is backed with quilt batting, the remainder of the bag fabric is quilted to give more body and hold the bag shape. The fabric used for this project was a medium-weight polyester linen type fabric.

The decorative panel can also be worked on the front panel of an envelope style bag or a pocket on the side of a larger bag.

Bag Panel _____

MATERIALS REQUIRED
Panel of bag fabric backed with batting
4 mm silk ribbon: Original colours:
Pink (2 shades) — No 91 & 93
Green — No 60
Small beads in pink (2 shades) and green

- Trace the pattern from the previous page on to thin paper and prepare the panel as described on page 23 centering the design carefully.

- Outline the design with whipped running stitch (see page 12) in chosen colours.

- Fill the inner petals with a mixture of shaded colonial knots and beads.

- Outline the centre petals and fill with green beads and colonial knots.

- Fill the centre with beads and/or colonial knots.

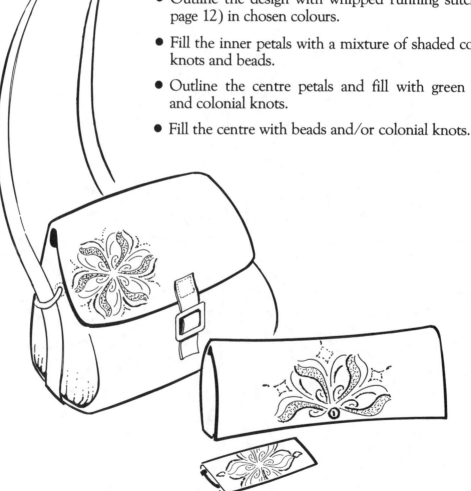

BOXES

There are a number of commercially produced boxes available for mounting embroidery. These are generally obtainable from specialist embroidery and craft shops.

An alternative is to find a wood turner who is willing to make boxes with recessed lids to accommodate the embroidery. The box pictured in the colour section was made for me by my husband and the embroidery is mounted on a plywood disc cut to fit the recess.

Often however, the most convenient and inexpensive way is to make your own fabric covered boxes which is not a difficult process.

To cover a round box you will need foundation templates to work with. You can try the following suggestions.

- Cut your own cardboard templates. Use a heavy duty tube (Postpak tubes are excellent) for the side and round discs of firm card for the base and top.

Cut three discs to fit just inside the tube, one for the base and one each for lining the base and top. Cut a fourth disc for the lid slightly larger in diameter than the diameter of the tube.

It is also possible to purchase a box kit containing these parts from some craft shops.

MATERIALS REQUIRED
To cover a box approximately 7.5 cm (3 inches) in diameter by 5 cm (2 inches) deep (see box pictured with daisy design):
You will need fabric and batting 50 cm x 35 cm (20 x 14 inches) ribbon for chosen embroidery design and spray glue.

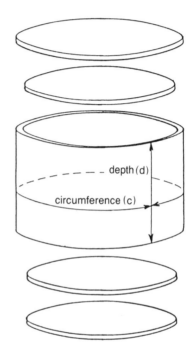

To construct a round box:

- Measure around the outside of the tube section.
- Measure the depth of the side.
- Fold the fabric on the *bias*, this is essential to achieve a good fit on the inside of the box, and mark out a bias strip to fit around the box using the measurements taken and adding 2.5 cm (1 inch) to the box circumference and 2 cm (¾ inch) to the depth.

The folded edge of the fabric will be on the top edge of the box side. Do not skimp on the bottom edge seam allowance as stretching the bias strip around the box decreases the finished width of the strip.

- Lay the four top and bottom templates on the remaining fabric and cut out circles allowing 2 cm (¾ inch) turnings. Note that when using an

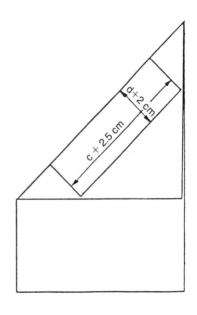

embroidered design for the top allow plenty of extra turning to ensure correct centering of the design.

- To pad the box lightly spray one side of all except the base disc with fabric glue and place them sticky side down on to the batting. Cut out each circle carefully. Cut a strip of batting to fit around the tube section covering both inside and outside surfaces. Spray the outside with glue and wrap with batting lining up the bottom edge of the batting with the bottom edge of the template. Trim the batting so that the short edges just meet but do not overlap. Pull the batting over the top edge of the tube stretching it firmly to remove as many creases as possible. Trim level with the base of the tube and whip stitch in place, stitching into the batting on the outside edge of the tube.

- Run a gathering thread using strong linen or buttonhole thread (dental floss makes an excellent substitute), around each circle of fabric. Centre templates, batting side down, on the wrong side of each circle. Pull up the gathering thread and fasten off securely stretching the fabric firmly around each template.

- Mark the side seam position on the bias strip by stretching it firmly around the box side and pinning in place. Remove the strip and machine the side seam using a small stitch setting. Trim the seam allowance and press open. Press up the seam allowance on one long edge.

- Fit the strip carefully over the side of the box having the pressed hem on the inside and lined up with the base of the side.

Pull the strip down over the outside of the box pushing the raw edge to the inside under the pressed hem. Working the fabric to keep it crease free and a very firm fit, hem the edges together along the bottom edge.

- Ladder stitch the unpadded base circle into place. Apply glue to the base lining disc and push into place.
- Glue or ladder stitch the lid lining inside the lid and place on top of the box.

An alternative is to use ribbon or braid to decorate the box side, in which case the bias strip can be pulled around to position the edges to be joined on the outside of the box and the turnings trimmed back so that the fabric just meets. Ladder stitch the two edges together and cover the seam with ribbon or braid.

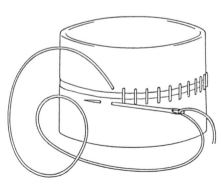

Boxes with recessed lids

- Cut a template in plywood or heavy card to fit the recess, allowing a small gap to accommodate the fabric. This allowance will depend on the thickness of the fabric used.

- Centre the template on the fabric. Cut out, leaving ample turning allowance to permit correct centering of the design.

- Spray the template lightly with spray glue and place sticky side down onto a piece of batting. Cut out carefully.

- For oval or round templates, using strong thread, run gathering stitches around the edge of the fabric cover. Pull up firmly around the padded template, adjusting to centre the design correctly. Tie off firmly.

- For square-sided shapes glue the seam allowance into place on the wrong side of the template, working alternately on opposite sides pulling the fabric firmly to remove all creases.

- Glue the template firmly into box top using a suitable adhesive.

Designs for boxes

The daisies, shown on a 7 cm (2¾ inch) diameter box, have been worked on pure silk and the buttercups shown on a 4 cm (1.5 inch) box have been worked on silk shantung. Both designs are exactly the same except for the size of the flowers. The daisies are worked in 2 mm cream (no 156) or off-white (no 1) with 4 mm green (no 20) for leaves. Daisy centres could be yellow, gold, tan or green. Buttercups are worked in 4 mm ribbon (no 15 or 120) with 2 mm green (no 20) for leaves. Centres are a deeper shade of gold thread for colonial knots.

Start with the centre flower then position six more flowers in a circle around the outer ring. Add green loop stitches between the flowers for leaves and feather stitch greenery around the outside circle if desired.

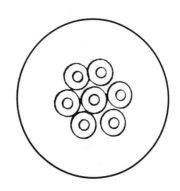

Wooden box _____

This design, worked on silk fabric, consists of poppies in 4 mm ribbon (no 2 or 28), three petal flowers in 2 mm ribbon blue (no 125) for outer petals and gold (no 15) for inside petals and pussy willow with stems in 4 mm brown (no 66) whipped running stitch and buds in cream 2 mm (no 156) single rosette stitch. Green leaves in 4 mm (no 20) and green feather stitch are used to fill in around the main design.

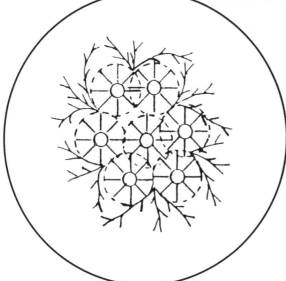

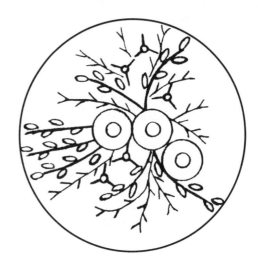

Metal music box by Framecraft _____

The top of this box has been worked on a fine deep green silk overlaid with olive green silk organza. It is essential to use very fine fabrics for this type of box otherwise the work is too bulky to be mounted correctly.

The design consists of briar roses worked in 7 mm ribbons in pinks (nos 5, 8 and 111) and straight stitch buds and leaves in 4 mm ribbon. The tiny bettle is worked in whipped stitch using 4 mm ribbon.

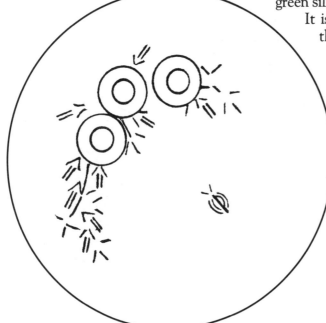

GREETING CARDS AND GIFT TAGS

It is possible to purchase the mounts for these in many craft shops, however, if you intend to make a number of them, it will cost less to cut your own.

Correspondence cards in various sizes, usually with fancy edges, can be purchased from stationers and can be used for place cards and gift tags.

To cut your own mounts you will need a sheet of heavy paper or thin card obtainable from art suppliers, a small craft knife and a template for the shape of cutout required. Either a picture frame matt board or the front section of a cardboard photo frame template, used for fabric covered photo frames, will make an ideal template.

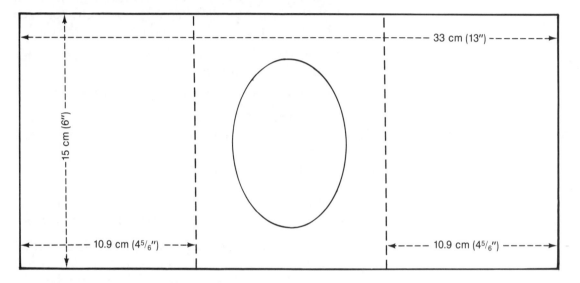

Cut the mount as shown in the diagram. Note that the third section is for folding behind the mounted embroidery. See page 33 for full-size drawings of the cut out shape.

Gift tags can be cut from the template given below.

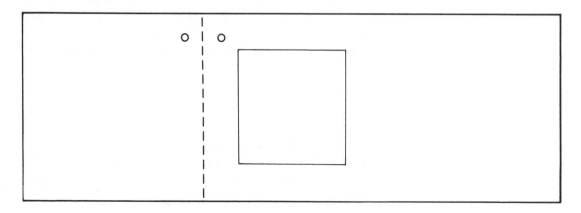

- Work your chosen design onto the fabric. As you work, position the card mount over the embroidery to check for size and positioning of the design.

- Cut the fabric to size, slightly smaller than the full size of the card front.

- Before mounting the fabric, cut a piece of thin batting to fit inside the window in the card.

- If you wish to cover the mount with fabric, proceed as follows using a suitable lightweight fabric:
  - Cut a piece of fabric the exact width of the front of the card but allowing 2 cm (¾ inch) for each of the turnings at the top and bottom of the card.
  - Glue the fabric into position on the reverse side along the top and bottom edge.
  - Cut away the centre opening, leaving a turning.
  - Clip the turnings around the curves to the edge of the opening and glue the turnings around the edge on the reverse side.
  - Finish the edges with fine braid.

- Position embroidery and glue into place, stretching it as the glue dries to remove as many creases as possible.

- Spread glue sparingly over the backing sheet section of the card, making sure that you glue the correct one so that the design is the right way up when the card opens from the right side.

- Carefully position the thin batting behind the embroidery over the cut out area and fold over the glued section to cover. The insertion of the batting helps to smooth out any slight creases in the embroidery.

The designs used on the cards photographed are detailed on the following page. However I am sure readers will be able to add many more. If you have a flair for painting try creating designs with fabric paint and adding just a touch of embroidery.

Roses and Fans

For the fans I used a very fine net lace 2 cm (¾ inch) wide and trimmed the bottom edge away to avoid bulk under the embroidery. The background fabric is silk Dupion.

- For each fan gather about 8 cm (3¼ inches) of lace to form a half circle and tack in place.
- Work a rose at the base of each fan; the original is worked in 4 mm ribbon, shades 49 and 50.
- Decorate the fans with tiny pearls, gold beads or colonial knots in gold thread. Add beads to the background as desired.
- A fine red braid encircles the opening.

The gift tag is one fan set on a square of fabric.

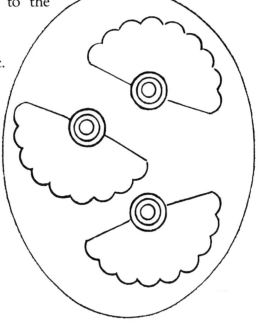

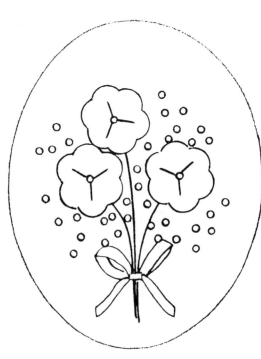

Lace Flower Bouquet _____

This card is worked on cotton batiste and a fine 1 cm (½ inch) wide lace used to form the flowers.

- For each flower gather about 6 cm (2½ inches) of lace into a tight circle and sew in position.
- Work three petal flowers (page 14) over the lace using 4 mm ribbon.
- Add stems and feather stitch greenery to the background. For an added sparkle overlay the green feather stitching with fine gold feather stitches.
- Add baby's breath using 2 mm ribbon and colonial or half colonial knots.

Gift tag. Work one lace flower with a little spray of baby's breath.

Wedding Card

Worked on silk Dupion with gold filigree net covering the face of the card. The design consists of apricot roses, apricot five petal straight stitch flowers with pale green centres, green and gold feather stitching and pearls. The edge of the oval is outlined with pearl edging which can be purchased by the metre.

This design could also be used on a prayer book cover or photograph album.

The gift tag is a single rose worked on silk overlaid with the net. Feather stitching and pale apricot colonial knots fill the background.

Additional designs for gift tags are carnation flowers (page 19) and charted designs for miniature cushions (page 48).

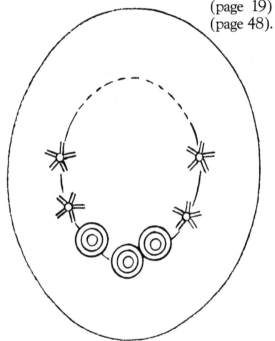

WIRED FLOWERS AND LEAVES

The flowers pictured on the wedding hat and in the corsage or hair decoration are made with a wired edge so that they can be shaped and moulded as desired.

MATERIALS REQUIRED

Suitable fabric — silk organza, georgette or any very light weight silk or polyester fabric, fine cotton covered wire and stamens — both obtainable from most craft and cake decorating suppliers, 2 or 4 mm silk ribbon to match the fabric, computer paper or similar for patterns, matching machine embroidery thread and a presser foot with a groove or hole designed to guide a cording thread, florist stem binding tape.

METHOD

To make leaves and petals:

- Using a marking pen that will show through the fabric, trace the required number of petals and leaves from the patterns onto the paper allowing at least 1 cm (½ inch) clearance between each one.
- Set up the machine with matching machine embroidery thread and the appropriate presser foot and a close narrow zigzag stitch.
- Place the fabric on top of the paper pattern, thread the thin wire through the hole or groove in the presser foot and, commencing at the base of each petal, work over the wire and stitch through fabric and paper around the outline of each petal.
- Cut out each petal leaving a 3 mm (⅛ inch) turning.
- Tear paper away carefully.
- Using silk ribbon cover the edges of each petal with overlapping whip stitches.

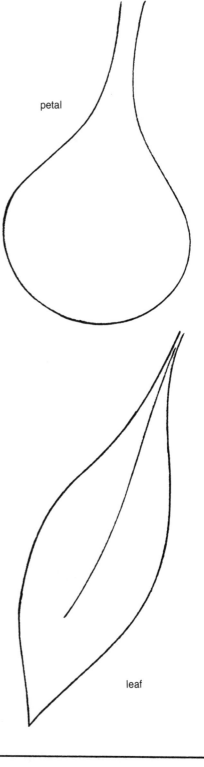

petal

leaf

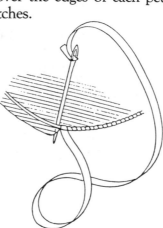

To construct a flower:

- Fold a small bundle of stamens in half and bind firmly with fine wire.

- Arrange four petals around the centre and bind together with the thin wire.

- Neaten the stem by binding firmly with stem tape stretching the tape as you roll the stem.

The flowers and leaves may be sewn on to the hat or a hairpiece as desired.

For a corsage arrange the flowers with leaves and bind together firmly with tape.

WEDDING HAT

The wedding hat is made by covering a purchased bucram shape.

- Cut a fabric pattern on the bias in calico or similar fabric to fit the shape.

- Bind the wired edges of the bucram shape using mercerised bias binding. Iron the binding flat then fold it over the edge of the shape and stitch firmly in place stretching the binding gently as you work.

- Cover the bucram shape with a very thin layer of cotton wool.

- Cut the covering fabric on the cross, using the pre-cut pattern as a guide, to fit the shape. Smooth the fabric over the cotton wool and stitch to the binding along the inside edge of the shape using herringbone stitch.

- Tack the lightly gathered veiling around the inside edge.

- Cut a lining on the cross, centre it inside the shape and hold in place firmly with pins or tacking threads against the curve of the shape.

- Turn under the edges and slip stitch in place gathering gently where necessary.

- The flowers and leaves may be sewn to the back section of the hat either before or after the lining is inserted.

BRIDESMAID'S ALICE BAND

The original band is worked on double georgette cut on the bias. Any fabric that would normally be used for a bridesmaids dress would be suitable. Cutting on the bias gives a smoother finish to the band.

MATERIALS REQUIRED
Fabric,
purchased alice band,
7 mm silk ribbon for embroidery and pearls.
Matching braid to neaten the inside of the band.

METHOD

- Carefully draw an accurate pattern of the band on to a sheet of paper. Cut out and double check against the band. Trace around this pattern onto a second sheet of paper.

- Cover the wrong side of the fabric with a layer of thin batting and lay the traced pattern on top *on the bias* and at least half the width of the alice band plus 5 mm (¼ inch) from the edge. Sew around this outline on the machine using matching thread (see page 23). Tear away the paper.

- Embroider with loop stitch flowers based on the briar rose but stitch a single pearl for the centre of each flower.

- Very carefully cut the batting away along the machine stitching line.

- Trim around the stitching of the band, allowing enough turning to meet and be hemmed together down the centre on the under side of the band.

- Sew the edges neatly, stretching the fabric as you work and trimming any excess fabric as you stitch.

- Glue a band of braid over the seam line.

join line

join line

HORSESHOE

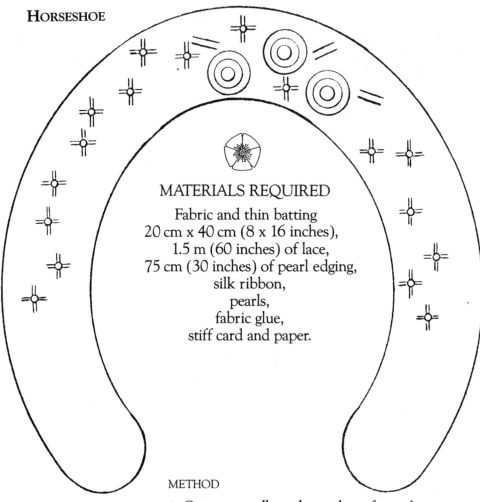

MATERIALS REQUIRED

Fabric and thin batting
20 cm x 40 cm (8 x 16 inches),
1.5 m (60 inches) of lace,
75 cm (30 inches) of pearl edging,
silk ribbon,
pearls,
fabric glue,
stiff card and paper.

METHOD

- Cut two cardboard templates from the pattern on this page and trace the pattern onto paper twice.
- Sandwich the batting between the paper pattern and the fabric and machine around the outline using matching thread. Repeat with the second pattern.
- Tear away the paper.
- Embroider one horseshoe with the design shown.
- Carefully cut away the batting along the stitching line. Trim the fabric away leaving a 2.5 cm (1 inch) turning outside the machined line.
- Clip the curves to the machine stitching, position the card templates over batting and glue the seam allowance down securely.
- Gather lace and stitch or glue around the edge of the embroidered horseshoe together with the pearl edging.
- Cut three or four 35 cm (14 inch) lengths of 7 mm silk ribbon and glue into position at the top.
- Glue the two sections firmly together.

SIMPLE IDEAS FOR QUICK RESULTS

All the ideas in this section are based on the carnations, page 19, which are made by gathering the ribbon into flowers that can be sewn or glued into place.

*Slippers*_____

Turn a pair of plain purchased satin scuffs into something special.

Three red carnations each made with 15 cm (6 inches) of 7 mm ribbon (shades 49 and 2) decorate the front of each slipper. Green loop stitch leaves tucked in around the flowers complete the decoration.

Christmas Tree Ball _____

To cover a 6 cm (2.5 inch) styrene ball:

- Cut four sections of fabric from the pattern.
- Score the ball with a craft knife into four equal quarters.
- Using the back of the knife, push the edges of each fabric section down into the cut stretching and smoothing the fabric as you work.
- Glue braid or lace over the joins.
- Make two green 2 mm ribbon rosettes on small headed pins and pin into the centre of two opposite sections.
- Glue three flowers, over the ribbon rosettes.
- Make two 4 mm ribbon rosettes, one with a hanging loop on pearl-headed pins for the top and bottom of the ball.

To make a rosette, pick up eight loops of ribbon on a pin as shown in the diagram. Stick the pin into the ball securing in place with glue.

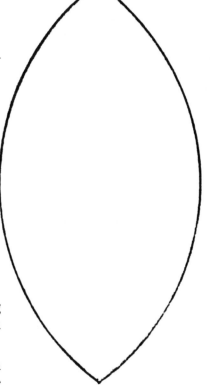

Heart _____

Using the small heart pattern on page 46, prepare two heart sections following the instructions given for the horseshoe, page 38.

- The heart is decorated with three cream flowers with red diamante centres glued over a rosette of 2 mm green ribbon. Use a threaded needle for making the rosette which can then be sewn into place. The ribbon ends are softly twisted two or three times before being glued or sewn into position at the base of the heart.

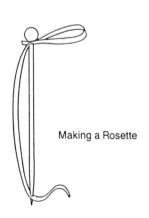

Making a Rosette

Earrings

Pretty earrings can be made by glueing carnations to earring mounts with an epoxy or similar strong adhesive (such as Araldite). Other flowers such as roses can be used in the same way.

First work them on fabric, then paint the back of the fabric with fabric glue and allow to dry. Cut out each flower with sharp scissors very close to the stitching, under the outer row of petals. Glue the flowers to the mounts.

Knitted Garments

Add an extra touch to knitted garments with silk ribbon. It has the coverage to show well on knitting but is light enough not to distort the garment.

A ruffled lace edging is added to the neck of the dress and front of the bootees using pearl stitch worked in 2 mm ribbon over the edge of a softly gathered french cotton lace.

Three petal flowers are scattered on the front of the bodice and the bottom of the dress and top of the bootees are oversewn with 4 mm ribbon. On this particular pattern, these edging stitches sit better when well spaced out.

ARMCHAIR SEWING CADDY

A pretty gift for any needlewoman, designed to hang over the arm of your chair and keep your work things neat and tidy while working in front of the television. Two pockets hold scissors and thread, etc, and a pin cushion protects your chair, and the rest of the family, from needles and pins.

This caddy makes an excellent class project as it can be treated as a sampler. Practically all stitches featured in the book are included in the design.

MATERIALS REQUIRED

50 cm x 112 cm (20 x 45 inches) of fabric
is sufficient for one caddy, if cutting your own
bias binding, or two if using purchased binding.
1.2 m (48 inches) of satin bias binding
for the outside edges.
1 piece firm batting 60 cm x 25 cm (24 x 10 inches).
Small quantity of stuffing for pin cushion.
Ribbon for embroidery.
1.15 m (46 inches) of fancy cotton entredaux
for simulating crazy patchwork.
1.15 m (46 inches) of satin ribbon to weave
through the beading.

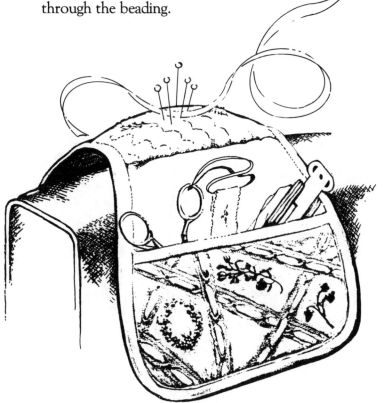

METHOD

- Trace pocket piece pattern (page 43) with all marked lines from page 44 or 45, onto paper twice. Prepare two pockets with all these guide lines marked as given on page 23. Tear away all paper.

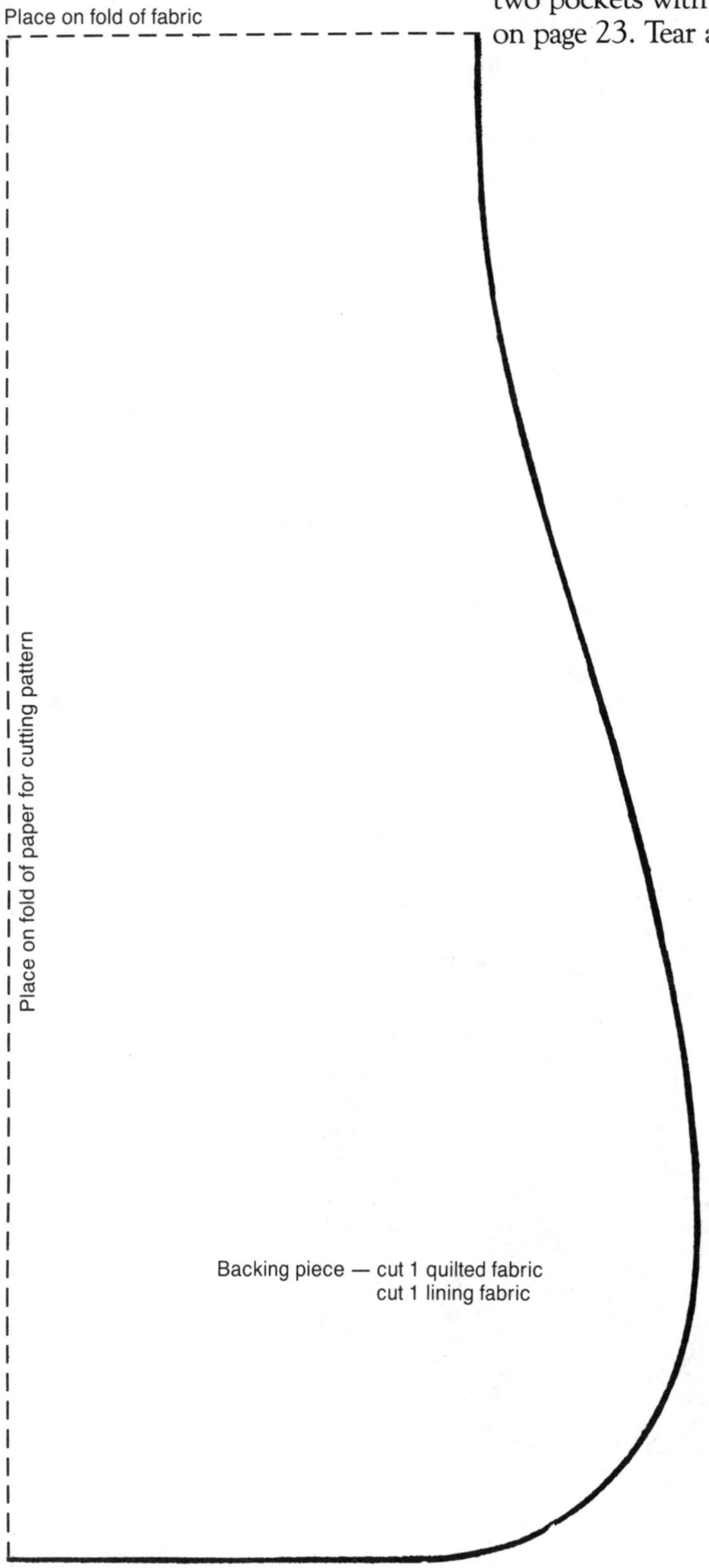

Place on fold of fabric

Place on fold of paper for cutting pattern

Backing piece — cut 1 quilted fabric
cut 1 lining fabric

- Trim edges away from beading and centre over machine stitching in strips, starting with the lines marked 1. Machine on both sides with a fine zigzag stitch. Thread with ribbon *before* adding strips marked 2. Repeat before adding the final strip 3. The diagram on page 44 gives the main outline of the designs, the positioning of the main flowers in each design together with the type of stitch used. The designs may be completed with your choice of tiny buds in single rosette stitch, colonial knots and feather stitch greenery.
- Embroider the pockets as illustrated or with any combination of flowers.
- Quilt a piece of fabric 60 cm x 25 cm (24 x 10 inches).
- Using the pattern on page 42 cut one backing piece from quilted fabric and one from the lining and pin wrong sides together.
- Cut two pocket linings. With right sides together match the top edges with the embroidered pockets and seam across. Turn pocket linings to inside, leaving a bound edge along the top.
- Position pockets at either end over the lining piece.

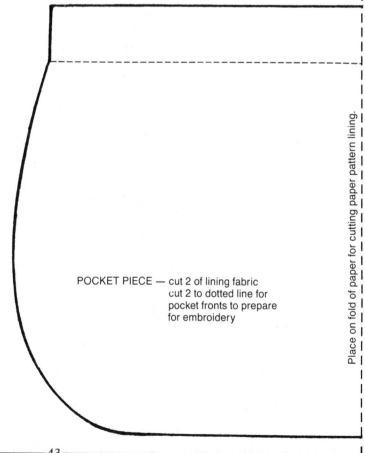

POCKET PIECE — cut 2 of lining fabric
cut 2 to dotted line for
pocket fronts to prepare
for embroidery

Place on fold of paper for cutting paper pattern lining.

● For the pin cushion, cut a piece of quilted fabric 15 cm (6 inches) square and decorate as desired. Seam into a tube and turn right side out. Centre the seam at the back and seam across one end. Stuff, keeping filling towards the centre until the pin cushion is mounted. Measure against the centre of the backing piece, matching closed end with one edge. Trim open end to fit the width of the backing piece and sew across the end. Pin in place.

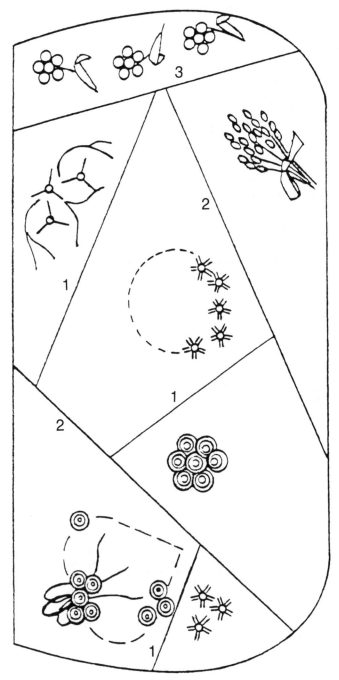

- Using a zigzag stitch, stitch right around the outside edge, taking care to hold the stuffing of the pin cushion away from the seam as far as possible.
- Bind the edge with a bias strip or purchased satin binding, stretching slightly around the curves.
- Work the pin cushion in the hands to distribute stuffing more evenly.

Pocket fronts show design area only, not including bound edges

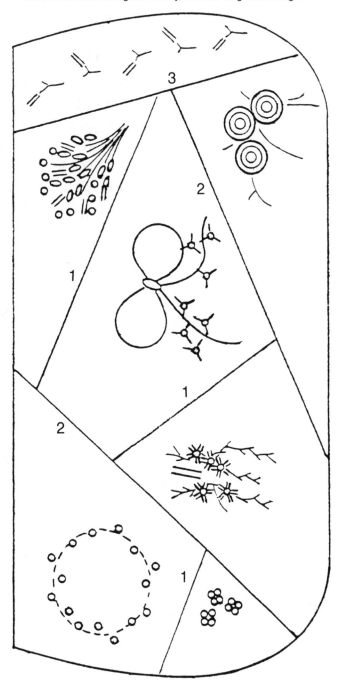

HEART

[Pictured on the front cover, in stages and on the back of the vest in the colour section.]

This heart could be used as decoration for clothing, cushion, quilt, basket lid, wedding album cover, picture and, no doubt, many other projects.

To work the heart, transfer the outline of the heart and the ribbons (page 47) to the fabric as detailed on page 23, backing the fabric with batting where necessary.

- Work the ribbons in whipped running stitch, working loops over the top of each other where they cross to give a more three-dimensional effect.

- Outline the heart with a single row of feather stitch.

- Add some side stems in feather stitch.

- Work roses or chosen large flowers.

- Now fill in with smaller flowers. Working a few of each type in a scattered design will help to give a good overall random effect to the finished work.

Small flowers used in the heart are:
— Straight stitch rose buds and four or five petal flowers,
— Pearl stitch four petal flowers,
— Rosette chain lavender stems,
— Colonial knot baby's breath.

VEST

The vest was made from a commercial vest pattern. Choose a pattern carefully. The only shaping in the pattern I used was in the side seam and two tiny darts at the back neck edge. Heavy dart shaping should be avoided as it may interfere with the final positioning of the embroidery. Patterns designed for patchwork garments are usually ideal. The garment photographed is embroidered with three different styles, the heart, on the centre back yoke area, the line design on the lower half of the front and back panels and the mock crazy patchwork design on the front yokes. Each of these styles could be used individually on a garment with great effect.

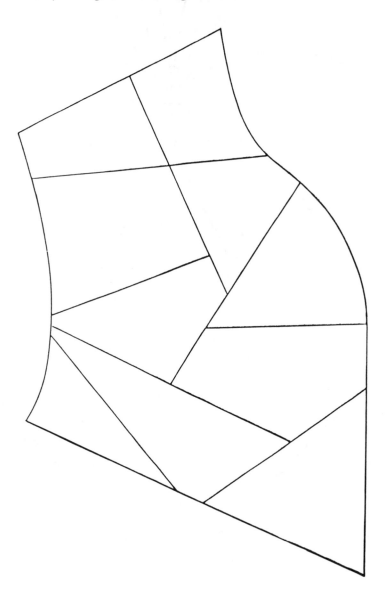

Lines of whipped running stick, pearl stitch and rosette chain are used to section the yoke, in place of the beading used on the sewing caddy. The positioning of the lines on the front yoke section are shown in the diagram on the previous page which has been reduced by 50%.

The line treatment on the lower half of the garment is worked directly over some of the quilting lines.

- To design your vest, cut out the pattern pieces in plain paper and draw the outlines of the design on the paper. Transfer design lines to the fabric pieces using the method given on page 23. All regular quilting can be done as described on page 23 without the use of this paper method.

- Tear away paper and complete any further quilting. In the case of the original vest the lower section is quilted with a twin needle in vertical unevenly spaced lines.

To make matching panels of unevenly spaced lines using the quilting guide, work on both fronts at same time and complete the same line on each front before altering the position of the guide.

Work the back in the same way starting at the centre line.

- Work all embroidery. You could use designs from page 44 and 45.

- Re-position the original pattern carefully and cut away any excess fabric.

- Cut out the vest in the lining fabric.

- Construct the vest and the lining separately by joining the shoulder and side seams. Place them wrong sides facing and tack or edge stitch together around the armhole and outer edges.

- Bind all edges with matching bias, satin bias binding or double fold braid designed for the purpose.

CHARTED DESIGNS

These designs are all worked with straight stitch on evenweave fabrics using the charts to determine the exact stitch position.

The miniatures pictured are all worked in 2 mm ribbon on a '25 count' (10 threads per cm, 25 per inch) evenweave fabric by Zweigart called Elfi.

The one inch (2.5 cm) squared pattern of the fabric is ideal for these miniatures making a perfect layout for the bedspread and the divisions between each square forming a perfect edge for pillows.

All three designs can be enlarged by working them with 4 mm ribbon on evenweave fabrics with fewer threads per unit width.

○　Colonial knots

○—○—○—○　Stems

— — — —　Leaves

————————　Straight-stitch flowers

(1) Rose Bud Design

Work rose buds as described on page 10, positioning them according to the chart. Stems are straight stitch thread and leaves are straight stitch ribbon.

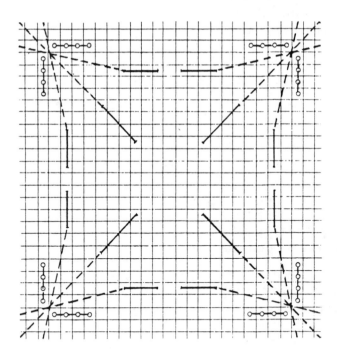

(2) Tiny Flowers

These are formed by working straight stitches in the form of a cross. A colonial knot in embroidery thread through the centre of the cross forms the centre of each flower. Add leaves using straight stitch.

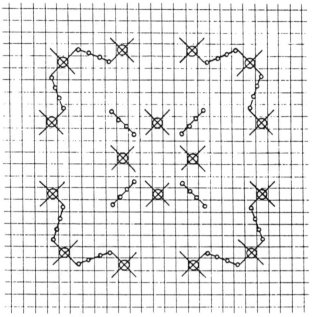

(3) Butterfly

It is essential to work the stitches in the correct order to achieve the best shape of the wings (as shown in the diagram).

Start with the front stitch of the front wing and work towards the back edge. For each of the back wings work the two centre stitches first then the outside stitches.

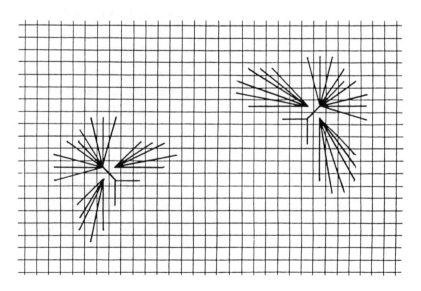

Cushions

It is easier to embroider several cushions at once. Leave a full square of fabric between each one for turnings.

 MATERIALS REQUIRED

Elfi, 13 cm x 18 cm (5 x 7 inches).
Stabilising fabric for embroidery
— silk organza, batiste or voile.
Backing fabric for cushions — voile or batiste
— two strips 5 cm x 22 cm (2 x 9 inches).
If plain evenweave fabric is used pull threads to divide the piece into 4 cm (1.5 inch) squares, centre the embroidery and cut the squares apart along the line of the pulled threads.

METHOD

• Back the evenweave fabric with the stabilising fabric.

• Work the embroidery and then press lightly.

• Cut out the cushions leaving a half square turning around all edges.

• Fold one strip of backing fabric in half and press firmly.

• Open out and place on top of the second strip, matching the edges. Using a long stitch setting, machine along the crease line.

• Fold *both* sections of the top strip to the right and both sections of the bottom strip to the left and press firmly.

• Place each cut out cushion right side down, centering it over the machine stitching down the centre of the backing fabric.

• Working from the wrong side of the embroidered panel, sew around the outside edge of the heavy dividing line between each square which is visible through the fabric. If using plain evenweave fabric follow a thread of the fabric for the machine stitching.

• Trim the seams and cut diagonally across the corners. Remove the machine tacking thread and turn the pillow through the centre back opening.

• Stuff lightly with wadding and ladder stitch the folded edges together.

Bed Quilt _____

The amount of fabric required will depend on the size of the bed and the positioning of the squared design on the fabric. There may be some wastage in order to position squares correctly. The top edge of the cover is folded to simulate the pillow area.

Plain evenweave fabric can be used and divided into squares by weaving with a heavy thread such as cotton perle number 5.

MATERIALS REQUIRED
Evenweave fabric 23 x 31 cm (9 x 12 inches).
Backing for embroidered area — silk organza, viole, etc.
Fusable hemming for turning hems.

METHOD

- Back the selected embroidery area with organza and tack in place.
- Work the chosen design. The ribbon may be carried behind the work on each individual square but not from square to square.
- Press finished embroidery lightly.
- Check the size carefully and trim where necessary, allowing half the width of a square for all turnings and fringing. Where the cover is required to fit between posts, measure the width carefully and centre the embroidered design.
- Fold under the top edge and seal with fusable hemming.
- Cut into corners if applicable and turn back hems as before. Seal the corner with a spot of fabric glue.
- Remove about twelve threads down the side edges and across the bottom for fringing.
- Fold the top section as indicated and steam press. Fold the sides and end to the back and press firmly to make the cover sit on the bed correctly.

Other uses for these designs are gift tags. Making decorative braid using 'Aida Band' (see the hat box). This can be used to decorate boxes, bags, booklets, covered books and photo frames or chatelaines (see photograph). The chatelaine featured on the colour page is made from 1.3 m (52 inches) of 2.5 cm (1 inch) 'Aida Band' backed with ribbon. Three 2.5 cm (1 inch) brass rings are used to weight the chatelaine at each end.

YOKES, COLLARS AND CUFFS

Silk ribbon work is very effective used on collars, cuffs and yokes.

It can be added to a ready made garment to make it more original as shown on the dress pictured. In this case the embroidery has been carried further to a touch on the sleeve, replacing the original button trim, and the plain buckle has been replaced with a fabric covered porcelain disc. The fabric used to cover the buckle came from the hemline when the dress was shortened.

Patterns for detachable collars are generally featured in commercial pattern books under 'accessories' or are available from speciality shops selling supplies for heirloom sewing.

Silk ribbon motifs can be added directly to the collar or embroidered onto a strip of fabric that can be used as an insertion into the collar or yoke of a dress, blouse or nightgown (see pink blouse).

The child's collar pictured is made using lace beading threaded with white satin ribbon to divide the basic yoke pattern into sections. The lace is applied over the collar fabric and the satin ribbon held in place with tiny colonial knots worked in 2 mm pink silk where the satin ribbon passes under the lace beading. The embroidered designs, given here, are worked in each panel in soft pinks and white (see back cover for close-up detail).

*Dress Buckle*_____

The design used on the buckle shown in the photograph is given here. The embroidery is worked onto fabric backed with batting and mounted over the porcelain disc by pulling the seam allowance to the back of the disk with a strong gathering thread round the edge. Tie off firmly.

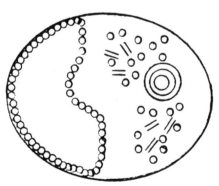

Cover the back of the disc securely with strong fabric. Adjust the belt length, if necessary, for the required waist size with sufficient overlap for the 'velcro' tape. Sew 'velcro' tape to the inside of one end of the belt and sew the disc firmly to the outside of this end. Sew the other side of the 'velcro' to the outside of the other end of the belt to give the required waist size.

LIST OF SUPPLIERS

Should you experience difficulty in obtaining the supplies mentioned in this book I suggest you contact the state crafts councils, where a comprehensive list of supply outlets should be available, or the local branch of the Embroiders' Guild where a similar service is normally available.

Addresses of the main offices in each state are given below. Local branches of the Embroiders' Guild can normally be found in the area telephone directory.

STATE CRAFTS COUNCILS

Crafts Council of Tasmania
77 Salamanca Place
Hobart TAS 7000

Crafts Council of Central Australia
PO Box 85
Alice Springs NT 5750

Crafts Council of NSW
100 George St
The Rocks
Sydney NSW 2000

Crafts Council of South Australia
PO Box 17
St Peters SA 5069

Crafts Council of Queensland
GPO Box 1867
Brisbane QLD 4001

Crafts Council of Victoria
7 Blackwood St
North Melbourne VIC 3000

Crafts Council of the ACT
PO Box 720
Dickson ACT 2602

Crafts Council of the NT
PO Box 1479
Darwin NT 5794

Crafts Council of Western Australia
GPO Box D178
Perth WA 6001

EMBROIDERS' GUILDS

Embroiders' Guild of the ACT
GPO Box 146
Canberra ACT 2601

Embroiders' Guild of Western Australia
29 Hubert St
Belmont WA 6104

Embroiders' Guild of NSW
2nd Floor Cusa House
173-175 Elizabeth St
Sydney NSW 2000

Embroiders' Guild of Queensland
149 Brunswick St
Fortitude Valley QLD 4006

Embroiders' Guild of South Australia
16 Hughes St
Mile End SA 5031

Embroiders' Guild of Tasmania
PO Box 158
Launceston TAS 7250

Embroiders' Guild of Victoria
170 Wattletree Rd
Malvern VIC 3144

Any queries for the author should be directed to:
Jenny Bradford
PO Box 5
Scullin ACT 2614
Australia
Phone: (06) 254 6814